W9-BDM-562

TERRIBLE

ESTATE AGENT
PHOTOGRAPHS

Andy Donaldson

◻ SQUARE PEG

For my family:
Dad, Lesley, Gordon, Angela, David, Claire, and Bram.

Published by Square Peg 2014

10 9 8 7 6 5 4 3 2 1

This collection copyright © Andy Donaldson 2014

Andy Donaldson has asserted his right under the Copyright, Designs and Patents Act 1988 to be identified as the author of this work.

First published in Great Britain in 2014 by
Square Peg
Random House, 20 Vauxhall Bridge Road,
London SW1V 2SA
www.vintage-books.co.uk

Addresses for companies within The Random House Group Limited can be found at: www.randomhouse.co.uk/offices.htm

The Random House Group Limited Reg. No. 954009

A CIP catalogue record for this book is available from the British Library

ISBN 9780024100915

The Random House Group Limited supports the Forest Stewardship Council® (FSC®), the leading international forest-certification organisation. Our books carrying the FSC label are printed on FSC®-certified paper. FSC is the only forest-certification scheme supported by the leading environmental organisations, including Greenpeace. Our paper procurement policy can be found at www.randomhouse.co.uk/environment

Printed and bound in Italy by L.E.G.O. S.p.A.
Design by Carrdesignstudio.com

Introduction

Inexplicably bad property photos. It's that simple.

Housing prices rise and fall, buyers come and go, decor comes in and goes out of fashion, but one constant remains throughout the property industry: photographic ineptitude and a lack of attention to detail. This book is a tribute to an important and unrecognised photographic genre, and to the artists who contribute to it so regularly, and with such low-quality offerings.

It's a tribute to estate agents who take photos of their own thumbs by accident. To agents who don't wait for your elderly relative to move out of shot. To agents around the world who, when presented with an unmade bed in a room littered with underwear think 'that looks great'. Click.

But out of these low standards can come great art. There is an indefinable beauty to these images, and not just in the unaccountably colourful curtains and vivid sofa coverings. The images presented here are more than just poorly-taken photographs. They are rich and compelling visual documents of a single moment in time, and for this we should be eternally grateful to estate agents the world over.

When I was a child, my favourite fairytale was the one about a front door doomed to gaze down on its original position from an upstairs window.

◁ Mirrors are a clever way of creating an incomprehensible vortex of confusion revealing absolutely nothing about what a property looks like.

△ So, how long has this place been on the market?

It's either a portered block or there's currently a delinquent urinating in the doorway.

Few architectural or geometrical features convey a sense of defeat and depression like a corner. Odd then that so many agents choose to make a feature of them.

Buyers would be well advised to securely lock the knife drawer.

Thanks, but I'll wait until we get home. It's only a 5-hour drive.

◁ To attract buyers, always decorate in neutral tones, avoid patterns and strong colours. Or make every room look like the inside of a migraine. Your choice.

▷ Whatever this furniture was doing before it was interrupted and photographed, I'm pretty sure it shouldn't have been doing it.

Throughout the history of estate agent photography, one iconic image of isolation and despair presents itself repeatedly. It has become known as the Garden Chair of Solitude.

That rarest of opportunities – all the joys of an overgrown garden full of weeds, with none of the disadvantages of having an actual house attached to it.

This property will be available as soon as the current tenants are done tidying up, which should be some time before the 2024 Olympics.

Fridge-freezers can become visibly depressed if left without the company of other white goods for a significant length of time.

Actually, I can probably hold on until we find one of those old-fashioned single-occupancy fellows.

Prior to coming on the market, this room operated as a drop-in centre for types of furniture that don't usually get to spend time with each other.

Sometimes the sheer magnificence of the vista is such that the only way to capture its full majesty is with the wide-angle panorama approach.

Design Trend Alert: kitchens are increasingly being built to accommodate those of us with particularly fast metabolisms. It has never been more important to wash your hands before preparing food.

The house is available for viewing, but ask nicely – it's very shy.

After days of waiting this agent's patience is finally rewarded. Weak with thirst, a pair of wild mattresses appear at the watering hole.

△ A testament to these austere times, this bathroom is constructed entirely from other houses' dead space, overhang, and stairwells.

▷ List of reasons why a room would have to contain a bucket and be almost entirely laminated:
1. Bad reasons.

Ah, the parties we used to have. Do you remember the one when we murdered everybody?

If those are nicotine stains, then that thing on the floor could very well be a lung.

All that's missing here is a figure in the doorway carrying an axe.

Presumably the idea being conveyed here is that if you *don't* buy the house, the agent can arrange for you to come to significant harm.

This house has already generated considerable interest,
particularly from fans of the popular new sport of Couch Tetris.

It's a start, but the more traditional approach of using floorboards would likely prove more successful.

Early viewing is recommended as there has already been considerable interest.
Mostly from horses.

Attention to detail is very important. For example, here the agent has dragged the body outside before taking the photograph.

This bedroom is a salutary lesson in starting your sentences further to the left.

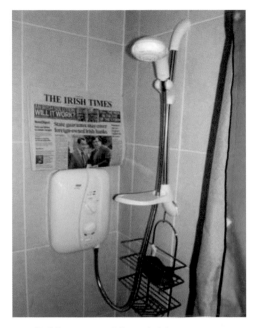

△ All things considered, it's a mystery why reading in the shower isn't more popular.

▷ A hangover from a childhood spent entirely indoors, the owner now carries an exit with them at all times.

In some societies, battery chicken farming led inevitably to the intensive rearing of children, often in the same buildings.

It was a wise decision not to include images of any of the other rooms, which presumably contained the sprawled and unconscious bodies of the current tenants.

A point-blank Mexican stand-off between two bright red sofas adjudicated by a television. In the world of feng shui, this is quite a low score.

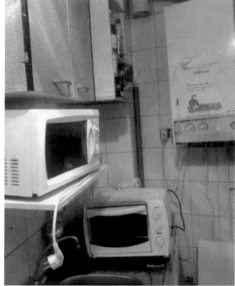

△ Contrary to popular belief,
most modern kitchen designers
positively encourage the interplay
of water and electrical equipment.

◁ Over time, agents learn
to identify one another by
their droppings.

Known as Old Faithful, this internal ventilation system grew from
a single washer planted by a local dignitary over 300 years ago.

We call this the blue room.

On a cold winter's night, there's nothing quite like a poorly executed drawing of a log fire.

Something about this picture suggests a certain lack of confidence in that stove.

There is a little-known psychological condition, the sufferers of which
imagine rooms to be far smaller than they actually are.

Buyers may want to reconfigure some of the more idiosyncratic plumbing.

Now that the condition has been recognised, more and more Garden Chairs of Solitude are using group therapy.

One can only admire the strength of character required to wilfully deny the existence of something as demonstrably real as a window.

Prospective buyers looking for somewhere depressingly unattractive to dump huge amounts of rubbish should rest assured.

Since the arrival of the internet, families spend less and less time
sitting together watching the fridge.

The garage features a man dressed as a pile of suitcases.

It could simply be some fibre-glass insulation, but the agent here also plays with the possibility that it's an armed Ewok.

Given that it's a trademark characteristic of the undead, I think we should be concerned about any estate agent who doesn't have a reflection.

The agent here is observing the age-old principle that if your face doesn't appear in a photograph, then you are not in the photograph.

The tragedy of early teleportation devices was the mess the unfortunate users made of the inside when they didn't work.

Even in otherwise empty rooms, pine chairs are notoriously nervous of mice.

The laws of estate agent photography dictate that even when a bin is being rejected and ostracised by the main items of furniture, one can't intervene. Nature must take its course.

As Rome fell, weeds grew between the marble pillars and nature reclaimed the ruins. Similarly, here we see nature slowly take advantage of man's lack of motivation when it comes to getting fit.

Let's be charitable and assume it's talcum powder.

Most people prefer using toilet paper, rather than attempting to paint over the marks.

Of course the danger of keeping your refrigerator in the bathroom is that someone mistakes a stool sample for chocolate mousse.

Viewing of this property is strongly recommended, preferably before it slides down the road and into the next village.

Built in Belfast in 1912, this flat was once famously described as 'unsinkable'.

This is a photograph of what I can only describe as a domestic horse.

We're told this dining room has also been the venue for several recent witch trials.

And this is the living room, where guests would be asked to perform for the entertainment of the current owners.

A tip: If a property doesn't have much going for it, try distracting buyers
by photographing something else instead.

There's no reason why agents should limit themselves to selling only the parts of a property that actually exist.

Modern software packages now allow agents to add artificial features to their photographs which are absolutely indistinguishable from the real thing.

Do excuse us. We'll come back later.

A tip: If someone has recently passed away in the presence of their loved ones and family priest, it's OK to rearrange the chairs afterwards.

A wonderful example of an agent taking their photography into the realms of abstract expressionism, in this case by creating an homage to Mark Rothko.

Ensure every day is a good day, by making it impossible
to get out on the wrong side of the bed.

Contrary to accepted wisdom, the best conditions in which to photograph a property are heavy rain and strong wind, thereby maximising the feeling of isolation and despair.

Custom
Moulded
Earplugs

**Grade 5
Moulded
Plugs**

Range of
colours
$92.00 per set

There is so much to cover here: earplugs can be custom made? They are graded?
They come in a range of colours? And they cost *how much*?
Oh, and this is a terrible estate agent photograph.

A rare glimpse of what zoologists call an arboreal trampoline.

Another foray into the world of post-impressionism. This time in tribute
to the Belgian surrealist René Magritte.

Generally speaking, a Zimmer frame without an old person attached to it isn't a good sign.

Seriously, put some clothes on. We're eating.

An interesting approach – focusing not on the view from the window,
but on the quality of the glass.

A particularly moving portrayal of a Garden Chair of Solitude. Forced to spend its remaining years as an outcast, it seeks solace in the company of non-specific building materials and dead foliage.

Sometimes estate agents hold up a mirror to the human soul to echo our fruitless search for meaning in a world bereft of comfort and love. They do it by sticking a chair in the corner of an empty room and taking a photo.

Another Chair of Despair.

Chair of Despair, a further example.

Convention usually dictates that standing units be attached to the floor, rather than the ceiling, but the human race didn't get where it is today by following rules.

He may be locked out, but something in that expression suggests
the agent hasn't heard the last of this.

Known as 'the fallback', in the absence of any attractive outside space, agents often resort to capturing a neighbour's garden from an upstairs window.

The garden has remained unchanged since being used in a Benny Hill title sequence in 1976.

For Sale. Owner last seen removing his jeans before jumping out of the window.

Rarely observed by humans, analogue television sets will often seek out their own kind for a chance to reminisce.

Sometimes an estate agent is able to capture not only the ordinary but also the extraordinary. In this case, an indoor blizzard.

It's rarely appropriate to use a property listing as an opportunity to market barbeque sauce.

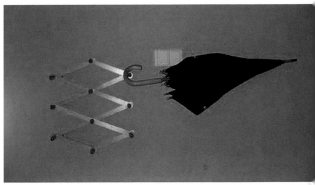

Every so often an estate agent will blur the boundaries between inept photography and conceptual art, and create something to baffle house-hunters and art historians for decades.

'That's all very well, but how would we get in? Oh, I see. . .'

Even with such a slim chance of recovery, it would have been better to have waited for the ambulance to leave before preparing to sell the house.

◁ One can only hope this property has remained unaltered since this photograph was taken. Which was during the Nixon administration.

▷ This is the room in which Uncle Ebenezer decided to spend his remaining days awaiting the Apocalypse.

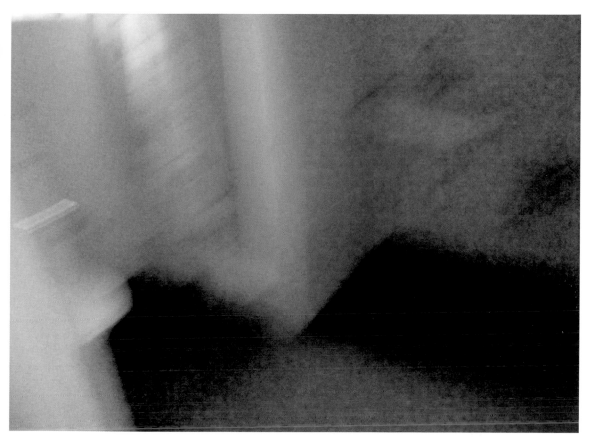

One has to admire the dedication of an agent who continues to take pictures
while in the early stages of a stroke.

The practicality of these bunk beds is compromised somewhat by the owners' inability to enter the room and use them.

Not all agents favour the traditional front door entrance. Here we see a rare example of what is known as the Commando Approach.

Triptych of Terribleness.

Good and bad. They should really be up by now, but it's encouraging
to see they were taking precautions.

Something of a David and Goliath situation. If David was a small bottle of bathroom spray and Goliath was a bath full of green slime. And if Goliath definitely won.

Classics of the much-maligned
Terrible Estate Agent Photography
sub-genre of Crazy Murderer Chairs.

It's either fungus or bullet holes. Either way, probably not a good thing.

◁ Nothing focuses the mind on the job in hand quite like the sound of other people's effluent as it flows past you on the way to the ground floor.

△ The heating system in this property not only kept the house warm, but was also used in the owner's unsuccessful experiments to create new forms of life.

For all their observational skills, estate agents still sometimes slip up. For example, here we have one attempting to photograph something that patently isn't there.

So, a set of amateur surgical instruments in a kitchen, and a cremation urn.
Only a cynic would suggest that there could be a connection between the two.

If the agent had subsequently decided to open the attic hatch, one suspects the following few seconds would have been spectacular.

If, on arriving to photograph a property, you find it has been wiped off the face of the earth, a hastily-erected marquee is unlikely to fool anyone.

Too good an opportunity to miss, the agent here has made a feature of a monster costume from an early episode of Dr Who.

The rain, the crate, the empty carton of milk. The remnants of a genuine contender for Most Depressing Garden Party of All Time.

This property features a fully fitted kitchen, as viewed here by a drunk man lying on the floor.

A rarely used technique: the agent attaches himself
to a high-speed ceiling fan and tries to capture the
entire room in one shot.

With a single click of the shutter, we are transported to a world where up and down have no meaning, where depth and height are alien concepts, and where people don't bother to arrange a viewing.

A playfully sentimental recreation of that old Austrian folk tale, 'The Hammock and the Bin'.

This property affords commanding views of the surrounding area,
which will give the buyer hours of pleasure pondering their own mortality.

Here the agent has broken with tradition and captured
the property in the style of a US cop show stakeout.

As appealing as this property is, there's always the danger
you might be collected and shipped to Belize.

The current owners are planning a garage sale, which is expected to raise around £4.

The beauty of pine trees is that they are evergreen (*sempervirens* in Latin), meaning that this property will be guaranteed no sunlight whatsoever, all year round.

Such was the beauty of this shower unit, all those who looked upon it were blinded and left to wander the earth looking for other property listings.

During times of economic or environmental crisis, it's common for householders to stockpile massive amounts of useless crap until such time as it becomes available again in Pound Stores.

In order to deter undesirable bids, it is sometimes necessary to scare buyers away using terrifying children's toys.

It's usually advisable to ask people to move out of shot before you take any. . .
Wait a minute. . .

As with the *Mona Lisa*, apparently this bed's pillows actually follow the viewer around the room.

One can entirely sympathise with the expression of confusion and horror worn by the fireplace.

Yes, but the chest of drawers is amongst the most racially sensitive we've ever come across.

This photograph was recently included in an exhibition entitled The Misery of the British Childhood.

The owners expect the carpet to produce at least another sofa and possibly some more curtains before the end of the year.

So new, in fact, it doesn't actually exist.

It's not a prerequisite, by any means, but if your grandparents end it all in a suicide pact it may be an idea to clear things up before the agent comes round.

This is what happens when you try to install a garden shed by catapulting it into position from 300 yards away.

Even to the untrained eye, this doesn't look like a very practical set-up.

No room is too small to allow the occupant to stare blankly at a wall from close range.

And this is where intruders will observe you from, while you do the washing up.

On the international market, idiosyncrasies of decor often betray the geographical location of a property as much as the address, such as with this house in Berlin.

A rare architectural feature this – a front door that is actually further away than the path's vanishing point.

It's said there are twenty-five things that will put a potential buyer off a house, and all of them are in this bathroom.

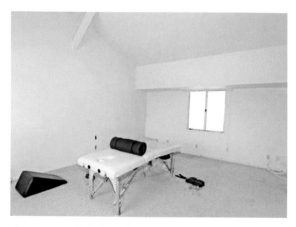

Decency dictates that we presume this room was only ever used for sports massage. Shall we move on?

Property comes with excellent storage space. Provided you only store waterproof objects.

If you get up during the night, you want to be sure you don't end up using the wicker basket instead.

The agent assures us that buyers will be able to open the kitchen cupboards when the ice melts in late spring.

Agents have to be increasingly wary of what is known as 'industrial photobombing'.

A rare example of what architectural historians refer to as a 'fertility window'.

The property is in an area popular with dog walkers: highlights can be enjoyed from an upstairs window.

In 2014 GoCompare.com Home Insurance surveyed UK homeowners and produced a definitive list of the

TOP 20 TURNOFFS FOR HOUSE-HUNTERS.

They were as follows, in ascending order of dreadfulness. . .

To you this is 'over-the-top'. To a Ukrainian dictator, it's pared-back.

Outdated decor, in the sense of prehistoric.

A professional cleaner could fix this up in no time, especially armed with
a flame-thrower and the authority to have the building condemned.

Yeah well. Another five minutes and I'd have had this place spotless.

Not so much General Untidiness as Field Marshal Chaos.

One way to deal with untidiness is to pass the contents of the room through a powerful fan. The drawback of this method is that it makes things immeasurably worse.

Sadly, paving over this garden only temporarily held it at bay.
Slowly, but surely, it is making a comeback.

One can't help but feel that whoever suggested a game of football
was being a tad optimistic.

We're assured that they *will* be plastic.

Maybe they're plastic, maybe not. They're almost transparent, what more do you want?

Easily solved. Concentrate on the floor instead.

All interest in the ceiling is thereby dispelled.

Outdated? Yes. But unwelcoming? No. Well. . . OK. Yes. That too.

13 Outdated bathroom

Maybe not 'outdated'. Let's just say 'past its best', at least for the time being.

Could be any of those. You go check.

Dirty protest house.

Agreed. Some things are best left to the experts. Like driveways, for example.

9 Small kitchen

Small kitchen, big fridge. Or is that a shower? Is this actually a normal-sized bathroom?

It's usually when a fridge reaches its late teens that the owners have to think seriously about up-sizing.

So small, in fact, there's barely enough room to sit and watch the microwave.

Who's to say
they're not
finished?

The gloom here is cleverly mitigated by the darkness and lack of light.

There's actually plenty of natural light, but it's currently eight hours away.

Not unless you park at high speed and over long distances.

4 Bad smells, including odours from pets

That would very much depend on whether or not the pets have been properly stuffed.

Guilty. Not a garden so much as a lack of indoors.

Perhaps so, but Christmas always kindled such fond memories.

1 Damp patches, stained walls and ceilings

It's all relative. Some people would kill for damp patches.